Colchester

Colchester

Martin Andrew

Waterton Press Limited

First published in the United Kingdom in 1999 by
Frith Publishing an imprint of Waterton Press Limited

British Library Cataloguing in Publication Data

Martin Andrew
Colchester

ISBN 1-84125-083-x

Reproductions of all the photographs in this book are
available as framed or mounted prints. For more
information please contact The Francis Frith Collection
at the address below quoting the title of this book and
the page number and photograph number or title.

The Francis Frith Collection,
'Friths Barn', Teffont, Salisbury, Wiltshire, SP3 5QP
Tel: 01722 716376
E mail: bookprints@francisfrith.com
Web pages: www.francisfrith.com

Typeset in Bembo Semi Bold

Printed and bound in Great Britain by
WBC Limited, Bridgend, Glamorgan.

Contents

Francis Frith 1822-1898

Introduction

Francis Frith: A Victorian Pioneer

Francis Frith, the founder of the world famous photographic archive was a complex and multitudinous man. A devout Quaker and a highly successful and respected Victorian businessman he was also a flamboyant character.

By 1855 Frith had already established a wholesale grocery business in Liverpool and sold it for the astonishing sum of £200,000, equivalent of over £15,000,000 today. Now a multi-millionaire he was able to indulge in his irresistible desire to travel. As a child he had pored over books penned by early explorers, and his imagination had been stirred by family holidays to the sublime mountain regions of Wales and Scotland. "What a land of spirit-stirring and enriching scenes and places!" he had written. He was to return to these scenes of grandeur in later years to "recapture the thousands of vivid and tender memories", but with a very different purpose. Now in his thirties, and captivated by the new science of photography, Frith set out on a series of pioneering journeys to the Middle East, that occupied him from 1856 until 1860.

He took with him a specially-designed wicker carriage which acted as camera, dark-room and sleeping chamber. These far-flung journeys were full of intrigue and adventure. In his life story, written when he was sixty-three, Frith tells of being held captive by bandits, and fighting "an awful midnight battle to the very point of exhaustion and surrender with a deadly pack of hungry, wild dogs". He bargained for several weeks with a "mysterious priest" over a beautiful seven-volume illuminated Koran, which is now in the British Museum. Wearing full arab costume, Frith arrived at Akaba by camel seventy years before Lawrence of Arabia, where he encountered "desert princes and rival sheikhs, blazing with jewel-hilted swords".

During these extraordinary adventures he was assiduously exploring the desert regions of the Nile and recording the antiquities and people with his camera, Frith was the first photographer ever to travel beyond the sixth cataract. Africa, we must remember, was still the "Dark Continent", and Stanley and Livingstone's famous meeting was a decade into the future. The conditions for picture taking confound belief. He laboured for hours on end in his dark-room in the sweltering heat, while the volatile collodion chemicals fizzed dangerously in their trays. Often he was forced to work in tombs and caves where conditions were cooler.

Back in London he exhibited his photographs and was "rapturously cheered" by the Royal Society. His reputation as a photographer was made overnight. His photographs were issued in albums by James S. Virtue and William MacKenzie, and published simultaneously in London and New York. An eminent historian has likened their impact on the population of the time to that on our own generation of the first photographs taken on the surface of the moon.

Characteristically, Frith spotted the potential to create a new business as a specialist publisher of photographs. In 1860 he married Mary Ann Rosling and set out to photograph every city, town and village in Britain. For the next thirty years Frith travelled the country by train and by pony and trap, producing photographs that were keenly bought by the millions of Victorians who, because of the burgeoning rail network, were beginning to enjoy holidays and day trips to Britain's seaside resorts and beauty spots.

To meet the demand he gathered together a team of up to twelve photographers, and also published the work of independent artist-photographers of the reputation of Roger Fenton and Francis Bedford. Together with clerks and photographic printers he employed a substantial staff at his Reigate studios. To gain an understanding of the scale of Frith's business one only has to look at the catalogue issued by Frith & Co. in 1886. It runs to some 670 pages listing not only many thousands of views of the British Isles but also photographs of most major European countries, and China, Japan, the USA and Canada. By 1890 Frith had created the greatest specialist photographic publishing company in the world.

He died in 1898 at his villa in Cannes, his great project still growing. His sons, Eustace and Cyril, took over the task, and Frith & Co. continued in business for another seventy years, until by 1970 the archive contained over a third of a million pictures of 7,000 cities, towns and villages.

The photographic record he has left to us stands as a living monument to a remarkable and very special man.

Frith's dhow in Egypt *c.*1857

COLCHESTER
"BRITAIN'S OLDEST RECORDED TOWN"

In many ways Colchester is a well-kept secret. Some people dismiss the larger towns of Essex as dull or too modern, but they have obviously never visited Colchester. It is a complete revelation, packed with history and with the evidence of all phases of that history around. The town is also superbly located on a ridge, with the valley of the River Colne to its north and east forming a natural defence.

Colchester must be one of the most historic towns in England, a belief certainly held by the borough council who call it Britain's Oldest Recorded Town on tourism literature and on main-route signs into the town. Unlike other towns that could make similar claims, Colchester has plenty of justification. Before the Roman conquest of 43AD, the town was called Camulodunum, the capital of the kingdom ruled by Cunobelinus, Shakespeare's Cymbeline. *Camulos* was a Celtic war god and *dunum* is a Latinised form of the Celtic "dun" or fort.

Colchester was the seat of a powerful and wealthy British kingdom that controlled large areas of south-east England. Its conquest was vital to the establishment of Roman power, and Emperor Claudius himself, in a brief visit to the conquered lands, came to Colchester where he received the surrender of numerous native tribes personally.

The town became a legionary fortress, its port at Fingringhoe playing a crucial role in supplying the troops and ferrying them and their supplies along the coast in support of the conquest. This phase ended about 47AD and by 50AD Colchester, now well behind the front line, became a *colonia* or settlement for retired legionnaires and the most important town in Britannia at that time. The town was laid out formally with streets running east-west and north-south, and enclosed by walls, probably timber at this stage. The Romans also built a great temple dedicated to Claudius who had been deified (as became something of a custom for emperors). This temple podium or platform survives under the castle which the Normans built around it, and from the plan it seems it had colonnades on three sides and was as good as anything in metropolitan Rome.

The Roman walls survive to a remarkable extent and are only substantially missing in the south-west corner of their circuit. They surround an area of 108 acres, a rectangle roughly 1,000yds by 510yds, and were built after 61AD, for reasons not unconnected with Boudicca. Due to the land dropping away northwards from the ridge towards the river, the northern part within the walls has steep streets descending from about 100ft to 25ft, which all adds to the character and interest of the town. The ridge also slopes from west to east, from about 115ft by Balkerne Gate at the west to 65ft at the east end of High Street, descending a further 40ft down East hill, beyond the walls, to the river bridge.

The highlight of the visible Roman remains, apart from the long stretches of 8ft-thick town wall and the temple podium, is Balkerne Gate. This was the great west gate, the entry to the town from the London road and the grandest of all the town's entrances. Much of it survives because the west end of this east-west axis fell into disuse, so the gate escaped the fate of the other Roman and medieval gates, such as the north gate, which was pulled down for road improvement in 1823, or the east gate which collapsed in 1651. The importance of the west gate was emphasised by a stone-faced triumphal arch with the vehicular carriageways each 17ft wide. The rest of the gate had a pedestrian way each side and a quadrant bastion, which contained a north and a south guardroom. The whole gate, 117ft across, was set forward from the line of the wall. Much of it survives today, including the south pedestrian way (still in use) and its guardroom bastion. The north bastion, pedestrian way and parts of the triumphal-arch foundations remain under (and supporting) the Hole in the Wall pub.

All over the town within the Roman walls, archaeological finds and excavations have helped build up a fascinating picture of the Roman years and the Castle Museum has many displays and artefacts that bring it all alive. I have dwelt at some length on the Roman phase of Colchester's history because it provides the skeleton of the town and has left a remarkable amount of stonework above ground. Colchester was also visited by the Roman Emperor himself who considered the capture of this capital vital to the success of the Conquest from 43AD onwards.

The next appearance on the chart of British history was less happy. Boudicca, or as she used to be known "Boadicea", Queen of the Iceni and daughter of King Prasutagus, ruled much of what is now East Anglia and rose in revolt after being flogged and her daughters raped by the Romans. The town with its mostly timber buildings was burnt, though the stone Temple of Claudius defied the Britons for two more days. The rebels swept on to burn more towns before their defeat and Colchester was rebuilt and walled in stone. It never fully recovered and although a prosperous town, Londinium, the more natural focus for the province, rapidly outstripped it as the premier settlement of Britannia.

During the Anglo-Saxon period the town was occupied at varying degrees of intensity, but the only physical reminder of these centuries is the fine west tower of Holy Trinity church, a mid-eleventh century landmark. It uses salvaged Roman bricks, septaria and stone from ruined Roman buildings, a habit continued by the Normans after 1066 when the town became a vast quarry for building materials. At the time of the Conquest the town was a prosperous one with seven priests. This presumably relates to the number of churches, including Holy Trinity, St Botolph's and St Runwald's, which was in the High Street near the town hall and was only demolished in 1878.

The Norman arrival led, as in other towns such as Norwich, to wholesale demolition to accommodate a castle with its baileys within the town walls. The great castle cleared the north-east sector of the Roman town and used salvaged Roman materials to build a great keep larger than the White Tower at the Tower of London, an inner bailey with ramparts and ditches, and an outer bailey spreading downhill as far as the Roman town wall. In 1096 the town and castle passed to Eudo Dapifer who founded St John's Abbey and St Botolph's Priory outside the walls.

During the Middle Ages and later, Colchester was a noted cloth-making town. This prosperity was marked by an increase in the number of parish churches to eight within the walls and eight outside, together with Greyfriars and Crutched Friars houses. Many fifteenth- and sixteenth-century houses survive in the town, though many were lost due to the Civil War and the earthquake of 1884.

In the later sixteenth century, Protestant refugees from the Spanish Netherlands (now Belgium) arrived and settled to revive Colchester's then-flagging cloth industry. Many settled in the Dutch Quarter, north of the High Street. Their presence reinforced the Protestantism of the town, which sided with Parliament in the Civil War of the 1640s. However, in 1648 a Royalist force seized the town, led by local Cavalier gentry. A bloody siege followed and after 11 weeks of bombardment and fighting the town fell. A great deal of damage was done by this siege: St Mary-at-the-Walls was virtually destroyed, as was much of St Botolph's Priory and almost all of St John's Abbey. Some of the town walls and many houses were reduced to rubble.

The town recovered and Celia Fiennes was able to write in 1698 that "The whole town is employ'd in spinning, weaveing, washing, drying and dressing their Bayes (baize)".

Earlier the castle had suffered misfortune and lost its two upper storeys, roofs and internal floors when it was bought for demolition by John Seeley in 1683. He gave up, but the effect was to reduce the dominance of the building in the town.

The eighteenth and nineteenth centuries saw much building in the town. This included public buildings, such as the hospital of 1820, the town hall rebuilt in 1846 and 1898, the giant water tower (Jumbo) of 1882, the barracks on the south side of the town, and the conversion of the castle to a museum, all of which contributed to the variety and interest of the town's architecture.

The twentieth century saw a massive expansion of the suburbs, the insensitively designed telephone-exchange tower block and the of-its-time Mercury Theatre. However, this went hand-in-hand with conservation policies, which repaired and restored the historic fabric, a process which is still continuing. Many areas have been rebuilt in a style that fits in with the scale of the older houses: areas re-knitted in sympathetic style, old lanes now with the buildings back, such as East and West Stockwell Street or St Helen's Lane. Even the shopping malls within the walls fit in well. Castle Park remains a fine lung for the citizens, but the road improvements, in particular Southway which cuts off St John's Green area from the walled town, are regrettable.

There is much to see and do, and the walled town is compact enough for any visitor to walk all the lanes and streets to get the flavour of its fascinating character. It is a deeply historic town with a range of superb museums, and this selection of old photographs captures some of this character and variety.

CHAPTER 1
A TOWNSCAPE TOUR
"THE TOWN LOOKS LIKE A THRIVEING PLACE" (CELIA FIENNES, 1698)

These views show the town from the 1890s to the 1960s and record both the many changes that have taken place and also, paradoxically, how much of the old town survives. The medieval street plan survives virtually intact, much of it based on the Roman town laid out in the first century AD. The main axis of principal roads consists of the Roman east-west artery, now the High Street, and one of the Roman north-south roads, now North Hill and Head Street. Other narrower and more winding streets and lanes lead off these, such as West Stockwell Street or Culver Street.

High Street itself was diverted from its true course by the castle inner-bailey wall and ditch, while at the west end beyond North Hill the road disappeared and Balkerne Gate became a backwater (a fact that ensured its survival, unlike the other town gates). The town was most densely built up south of High Street and along North Hill and Head Street, while the area west of the castle baileys was also heavily populated.

Outside the walls medieval housing and buildings spread along the road north from North Hill over the River Colne, along East Hill beyond the east gate, along East Street beyond the Colne, and to the south around St Botolph's Priory and St John's Abbey.

The grandest buildings are found along High Street and on East Hill. The High Street views show the width of the street well, an effect partly achieved by demolishing encroaching market buildings on the slope up to the town hall. High Street and Head Street, mostly rebuilt or refaced in brick, present a late-eighteenth and early-nineteenth century character with flat fronts with sash windows. Only the occasional medieval or sixteenth- and seventeenth-century timber-frame building, such as The Red Lion, appears in these streets.

In the narrower streets more timber-frames survive, particularly in the Dutch Quarter, the streets north of High Street, where the former Angel Inn and The Stockwell Arms are found; or at the foot of East Hill and in East Street, where the splendid Siege House is located. Many more remain concealed by plaster and render, such as those around Schere Gate or in West Stockwell Street. Georgian brick is also everywhere and east of the castle on High Street and East Hill are some fine mansions, such as Hollytrees Museum and The Minories.

Of Victorian and nineteenth-century note is the Eaglegate Brewery of 1888 down East Hill, as well as some good commercial buildings, pubs and shops in the main streets. Also of note is the town hall, the fine Arts and Crafts library attached to it in West Stockwell Street, Jumbo (the water tower) and the former Cup's Hotel, which represent a grander style towards the end of the nineteenth century and into the Edwardian years.

The walled town has always been delineated by the River Colne to the north and east, but the twentieth century has now provided its own river to the west and south. A tarmac one and just as difficult to cross: Balkerne Hill and Southway, the former giving fine views of the Roman wall, perhaps the best since the Middle Ages!

HIGH STREET, 1891.

A dignified streetscape of Georgian and early Victorian frontages climb towards the old town hall in the centre of the view, its blank side exposed since 1878 by the demolition of St Runwald's church. Beyond is Jumbo, the water tower erected in 1882.

28208

HIGH STREET, 1901.
By 1901 the magnificent town hall with its 160ft tower, a florid, exuberant baroque building started in 1896 and designed by Belcher, was complete. Its stolid neo-classical predecessor of 1846 had been pulled down in 1894 because it wasn't grand enough for the aspirations of the corporation.

47650

HIGH STREET, 1934.

By 1934 the streetscape is more cosmopolitan with the Art Deco Marks and Spencers on the left, and the Edwardian Grand Theatre, now the Hippodrome, and the classical-style pub, now the Faunus and Firkin, on the right replacing the simple Georgian flat-fronts.

HIGH STREET, 1892.

This view shows how Jumbo the water tower dominates views in the town. The Cup's Hotel on the right has now gone, as have several of the buildings on the left and those in front of Jumbo, mostly not for the better.

HIGH STREET, 1892. 31518
In this direction looking east, the most startling change is the loss of the church with its dominating crocketted spire. St Nicholas, a medieval church largely rebuilt in decorated Gothic style in 1876, was demolished in 1955 to make way for a three-storey Co-op store of considerable mediocrity.

MUSEUM STREET, 1921.

70360

This charming lane leads from the castle gates to the High Street, but is now marred by flat-roofed, two-storey 1960s shops on the left and the view is now terminated by the empty Co-op store, rather than St Nicholas' church tower and spire.

WEST STOCKWELL STREET, *c.*1960.   C136050

The Stockwell Streets are the heart of what is known as the Dutch Quarter, a recent name for the area in which Flemish weavers settled around 1600. This view has the old Angel Inn on the left and the former library; beyond is the wonderful town hall.

WEST STOCKWELL STREET, *c.*1960.   C136051

This view looks in the opposite direction downhill to the heart of the Dutch Quarter, past the former Angel Inn dating from about 1450 and now well-cared for by a firm of solicitors. Beyond the horse chestnut tree is the wall of St Martin's churchyard.

WEST STOCKWELL STREET, 1904. 52349

All except the building on the far left survive now, although Daniell and Sons is now The Stockwell Arms pub. These are some of the finest fifteenth and sixteenth-century, rendered, timber-framed and jettied buildings in Colchester.

NORTH HILL AND MARKET, 1892. 31522

North Hill climbs towards High Street, just beyond St Peter's church tower seen in the distance. The houses on the right have long gone and have been replaced by a wide modern road whose only virtue is the exposure of the Roman wall formerly concealed behind the houses.

NORTH HILL, 1891.   28211

The fine Georgian tower of St Peter's church was built in 1758, replacing the medieval one which was damaged by an earthquake in 1692. The gabled building on the left was demolished in the 1920s for The Waggon and Horses pub.

NORTH HILL, *c*.1960.   C136097

The road descends northward to Middleborough beyond the line of the Roman wall. This view gives a good idea of the height of the main part of the town on its ridge above the River Colne valley.

NORTH BRIDGE, *c.*1960.

C136022

The houses of Middleborough grew up beyond the town walls and the north gate, which was demolished in 1823. The present cast-iron North Bridge over the Colne was built in 1843 and widened in 1903-08. The timber-framed cottages reflected in the water are seventeenth century.

HEAD STREET, 1891.

28212

Looking north to the junction with High Street, all the taller houses on the right were replaced by what is now Debenhams department store. Amid the Georgian and early-nineteenth century fronts on the left, a tall interloper of the 1880s survives.

ST MARY-AT-THE-WALLS CHURCH, 1921.   70372

In this view St Mary's is situated above a quiet lane in the old town. Today it peers over the western Roman wall exposed by the demolition of all these cottages and into the roaring gulch cut by Balkerne Hill, a dual carriageway stretch of the western bypass or ring road.

CROUCH STREET, c.1955.   C136009

Where the bus meanders westward the dual carriageway of Balkerne Hill removed a number of buildings on each side of the road on its noisy way to the Southway roundabout, cutting Crouch Street into two. The best house in the street is No 22 on the left, which is Georgian and dated 1763.

TRINITY STREET, 1921.   70361

The lamp on the left lights the alley to Tymperleys, a superb late-fifteenth century timber-framed house, now a clock museum. Beyond Holy Trinity's Anglo-Saxon tower, the town hall's mighty tower closes the vista superbly: another example of its powerful contribution to the townscape of Colchester.

ST JOHN STREET, 1921.   70363

Although many buildings in St John Street and Vineyard Street have been lost, this wonderful group of jettied buildings survives, clustering up to Schere Gate, possibly a medieval gate through the town wall. Much has changed hereabouts and the dual-carriageway southern bypass, Southway, is a mere 50 yards to the south.

SCHERE GATE, 1908.   60778
This closer view shows the steps under the gateway with the Roman wall incorporated in the house. The rendered buildings have Georgian sash windows but they conceal the medieval timber-framed structures of houses built immediately outside the wall and its gateway. The one on the right now has a shopfront.

EAST GATE, *c.*1955.   C136014

To the east, beyond the town wall, houses grew up along the road out of the town as it descended off the ridge towards the River Colne. The grander houses are at the top of the hill, including No 86 on the left, an ornate stucco mansion of about 1840.

EAST GATE, *c.*1955   C136015

Looking uphill towards the town, the Esso garage and hotel on the right have been replaced by an intrusive and modern petrol station. The high roof beyond the tree on the right was the former Eaglegate Brewery, rebuilt in 1888.

OLD HOUSES, EAST STREET, c.1955.
This view from the Ipswich Road junction shows the fine range of mainly medieval houses leading towards the bridge over the Colne. The row terminates with the late-fifteenth century Siege House, while the pyramid roof peeping over the roofs belongs to Marriage's Watermill, now an hotel.

C136001

CHAPTER 2
THE TOWN OF COLCHESTER:
ROMAN WALLS & CIVIC SUBSTANCE

For a while Colchester was the chief town of Roman Britain. In 50AD, soon after the invasion of 43AD ordered by the Emperor Claudius, a colonia was established, a town for retired legionary soldiers. Its importance was a reflection of its earlier British history, for it had been the capital of King Cunobelin, Shakespeare's Cymbeline, and was known as Camulodunum. Colchester's Romano-British supremacy was short-lived, for in 61AD Queen Boudicca of the Iceni rose against Roman rule and sacked the town. Although it recovered to become a prosperous town, its pre-eminence passed to Londinium.

However it had a great temple dedicated to the God-Emperor Claudius, a forum, amphitheatre and many houses lining streets that still form the basis of the town's layout. The most spectacular Roman remains are undoubtedly the town walls, which survive for the most part (to varying heights). The walls enclose a rectangle roughly 1,000yds by 500yds and the best stretches are those along the west side and within Castle Park.

Also on the west side is the Balkerne Gate, originally the west gate to the town but saved by the section of road west of North Hill falling out of use. Here the carts, chariots and horsemen passed through a stone-faced triumphal arch with two roadways 17ft wide. Beside this there were pedestrian gates six feet wide and bastions for guards on each side. The south guardroom and pedestrian way survive, but the roadway arches were removed and replaced by a wall, probably in the eighth century. The north arch and bastion now support The Hole In The Wall pub, which some years ago demolished part of the bastion to improve the view for its patrons!

Colchester is remarkably lucky in its Roman remains and, enclosing 108 acres, is small enough to walk round and get the feel of the walled town. While doing so it is impossible to ignore two of the modern town's largest monuments: one practical, the other civic. The former is the great 105ft water tower erected beyond the west end of High Street in 1882 and which soon acquired the nickname of Jumbo. In the 1890s the old town hall, in fact only erected in 1846, was thought insufficient for the dignity of the Victorian corporation and was replaced by Sir John Belcher's splendid Baroque-style design. In warm orange-red brick with stone dressings and surmounted by a 160ft tower, Colchester's town hall is a confident and supremely satisfying building. Ornate and rich, the building or at least the tower is seen or glimpsed from all sorts of locations in and around the town, some expected and some a surprise.

Other buildings picked out for this chapter include some of the town's finest timber-framed, late-medieval structures, displaying a wealth of jettied upper storeys, carved dragon posts and close-studding. Of the two public buildings chosen, one survives and prospers: the Essex County Hospital of 1820; while the other, the Essex Hall Hospital, has been demolished and is now commemorated by a street name only. The latter started life as a railway hotel before failing and being turned into an asylum.

OLD ROMAN WALL, 1892.   31531

Virtually all the west side of the town's Roman wall survives and it now flanks the dual carriageway of Balkerne Hill, fully exposed to view. The good Georgian pub (The Hole in the Wall) at the end of this stretch of wall actually sits on the remains of the north bastion of the Balkerne Gate.

ESSEX COUNTY HOSPITAL, 1892.   31540

The original parts of the hospital were built by public subscription in 1820, while the portico was added in 1825 and further extended in 1839 and the diagonal wings were added in 1879. Although the site is much expanded now and the lawns have been turned into a crowded carpark, the original buildings survive intact.

THE ASYLUM, 1891.   28217

Heavily influenced by the baroque style of Hawksmoor, this fine building, now demolished, was built as the Victoria Hotel in 1843 to cash in on the arrival of the railway. Not a success, it closed to re-open in 1849 as an Asylum for Infant Idiots, later more tactfully renamed the Essex Hall Hospital.

THE WAR MEMORIAL, c.1960.   C136064
This grand war memorial by Henry Fehr was erected in 1923 on a site formed by the demolition of a number of houses at the east end of High Street, which visually linked the street to East Hill – a considerable error of judgement in townscape terms.

TOWN HALL, 1902.   48298

The wonderfully over-the-top Baroque town hall is a triumph for the town and much better than the pallid
neo-classical one it replaced. In Sir John Belcher the corporation found an architect to undergird its civic pride.
Newly complete here, its streetscape impact can be fully appreciated.

THE MOOT HALL, TOWN HALL, 1904. 52344
The monumental scale of the town hall is
continued inside in the Moot Hall, a linguistic
link to Anglo-Saxon Colchester. Here giant
fluted Corinthian columns support a massive
cornice and a segmental roof with the organ
behind the dais.

THE WATER TOWER, 1907.   57541
Designed by Borough Surveyor Charles Clegg,
the 100ft building was opened amid great
civic pomp in 1882. Like the town hall tower, it
dominates for miles around and is also in a
monumental Baroque style. The pond is now
replaced by the uncompromisingly modern
Mercury Theatre, built in 1972.

THE OLD SIEGE HOUSE, *c.*1955.   C136021

Colchester was besieged by Parliamentarians in 1648 and Siege House, a late-fifteenth century jettied mansion was peppered by Royalist shot: you can see where by red rings around the bullet holes. Immediately west is the river, which formed the front line during the bloody 11-week siege.

THE FORMER ANGEL INN, *c.*1960.   C136073

This fine jettied and timber-framed building of about 1450 has superb carved timber tracery to some windows: a rare survival in domestic architecture from this period. The jetty brackets have carved angels supporting them and the left-hand door originally led into the "screens" passage of the inn.

NOS 11&12 WEST STOCKWELL STREET, *c.*1960. C136040

These Georgian brick-fronted houses were lived in by Jane and Ann Taylor from 1796 to 1811. Writers of children's verse, their most famous poem is "Twinkle, Twinkle, Little Star", as commemorated by a brown corporation plaque.

THE RED LION HOTEL, *c.*1960. C136038

This medieval inn with characteristic ranges on each side of the yard reached through the carriageway, was in fact a fifteenth-century house converted to an inn about 1500. With the upper storeys and the eaves jettied, the rear yard, also with jetties, now leads to the Lion Walk shopping mall.

THE ROSE AND CROWN HOTEL, *c.*1955.

A range of fifteenth- and sixteenth-century timber-framed houses, some jettied, the Rose and Crown follows the curve of a lane linking Ipswich Road and East Street. Since the 1950s it has been fully restored but its setting is not wonderful, as it is marooned amid new development.

THE CUP'S HOTEL, 1892.

31521

The hotel with its six gables and ponderous style replaced a stuccoed eighteenth-century building, but has now gone to be replaced by the bland misjudgment of 1970s Greytown House. To the right is the 1846 pilastered previous town hall: somewhat less dominant than the current exuberant town hall.

Chapter 3

Colchester Castle & its Park
The Fortress on the Colne

The astonishing thing about Colchester Castle is the fact that it is built around the podium of the great Roman temple dedicated to the God-Emperor Claudius, whose legions had begun the conquest of Britain in 43 AD. This vaulted structure, roughly 80ft by 110ft, has two parallel stone vaults and massive walls that formed the platform for the temple which was the centrepiece of the colonia for retired legionary soldiers. It was burnt down by Queen Boudicca (or Boadicea) of the Iceni in 61AD, along with the rest of the town, as a symbol of Roman oppression. The temple was quickly rebuilt and survived in some form until the Norman Conquest, when the walls above the podium were then demolished. The podium was kept, though, and this perhaps accounts for the great size of the Norman keep, which was erected around it in the later eleventh century.

The keep's similarity to the Tower of London's White Tower is striking and some believe it was built by the same designer, Gundulph, Bishop of Rochester. The chief difference is merely one of scale. Colchester keep is 151ft by 110ft, compared with the Tower of London's 117ft by 107ft. It has massively thick walls and a "battered" or sloping plinth specifically intended to discourage undermining. Originally it was 90ft high with two more storeys, so it now appears much squatter and less menacing than when first built.

Set within a ramparted and ditched inner bailey with a steeply sloping outer bailey bounded by the old Roman wall, the castle occupied the bulk of the north-east section of the town, clearing Anglo-Saxon housing in the process. Now within a park with its military teeth drawn, its north rampart and ditch incorporated in walks and rose beds, the turbulent past of the castle is difficult to visualise.

Turbulent it was, though, and the castle was even captured by the French in 1215 and again in 1217. By 1250 it was used as a prison and in the 1550s held Protestants in the reign of Mary, at least 15 of whom were burned at the stake, and Catholics under Elizabeth I. In 1648, it played a key role in the great siege of the town that lasted for 11 weeks before the Parliamentary army retook it from the Royalists.

The next and most catastrophic event befalling the castle was its sale to John Wheeley in 1683, who set about demolishing the massive structure for its materials. He succeeded in removing the top two storeys, all the floors and roof before giving up. In the eighteenth century it resumed its career as a prison (apparently it was an atrocious and dank one, too), until closing in 1835. After this, in 1855, it was a home for the town's museum and in 1892 the grounds were opened as a park for the citizens of Colchester. Finally, in 1920, Viscount Cowdray bought the park and the castle and gave it to the town.

It is still a wonderfully evocative building and it is a source of wonder that the massive structure we see today is only half its full height. Limewashed as it would have been, it must have dominated the countryside from its ridge and been one of the wonders of Essex.

THE CASTLE FROM THE SOUTH-WEST, 1891.   28215

In 1891 the castle keep had been the town museum for 30 years and the owner, Charles Round, allowed the townspeople access to the grounds on an informal basis. Note how the surrounding ground level almost conceals the great "battered" or sloping plinth and the creeper-clad walls.

THE CASTLE FROM THE SOUTH-WEST, 1892.   31524

One year after the 1891 view, the grounds have been opened up, hedges removed and more lawns planted. Although still owned by Mr Round, the grounds were opened by the mayor as Castle Park for the benefit of all the citizens of Colchester.

THE CASTLE ENTRANCE, 1934.

The area in front of the main entrance had been excavated in 1933 and visitors now climb wooden steps to view the interior, itself roofed-over in 1932 after over two centuries unroofed. The excavations revealed complex outworks to protect the entrance, as well as a chapel, possible Anglo-Saxon.

THE CASTLE FROM THE SOUTH-EAST, *c.*1960.

This view shows the bridge into the castle, recently renewed, and the apse or semi-circular projection. This, like the one at the Tower of London, housed the castle chapel. In fact only the sub-chapel survived, because the chapel in the storey above was removed during the 1683 demolition.

THE CASTLE FROM THE NORTH-EAST, 1892.

This view shows the new trees planted in the park, which was opened in that year. The ground level conceals much of the battered plinth, the small doorway now being reached up a flight of timber steps.

THE CASTLE FROM THE NORTH-WEST, 1891. 28216

This view was taken before the grounds opened as a public park and it shows not only the high ground level around the keep but also the poor state of the stonework. It was not until 1920 that Lord and Lady Cowdray bought the castle and grounds, and donated them to the town.

THE OLD PRISON DOOR, 1908. 60775

The castle had been used as a prison since the thirteenth century and prisoners included Protestant martyrs under Mary Tudor, and Catholics under Elizabeth I. In private hands it was leased by Charles Gray as the county jail in 1734, closing in 1835 following years of complaint about its revolting conditions.

PARNELL'S CELL, 1908. 60774

This refers to James Parnell, the first Quaker martyr, rather than the later Irish patriot. In fact the view is incorrect, for he was imprisoned in "The Oven", a cramped cell next to the great staircase and near the well in the diagonally opposite corner of the keep.

THE CASTLE INTERIOR, 1895. 35504
The roof and floors had been removed when the upper two storeys of the keep were demolished after 1683. This view can no longer be seen, as a new roof and floors were installed in 1932, due to water damage to the Roman vaulted basements.

CASTLE WALLS AND TOWN HALL, 1907. 57536
This view shows the wall walk, originally passageways in the thickness of the third storey of the higher keep. Jumbo can be seen to the right of the town hall's soaring tower. The lower archway of the three within the castle was a fireplace.

CASTLE PARK, THE MAYOR'S WALK, 1898.   41501

After the park's formal opening in 1892, trees were planted and trim lawns made. The castle was also repaired and the ground outside lowered to expose its "battered" plinths. This is the Mayor's Walk along the north side of the keep and within the inner bailey.

THE CASTLE GROUNDS, c.1960.   C136086

By 1960 some of the 1890s trees were fully mature. Subsequently there has been much thinning and opening up to the benefit of the castle's setting. This view is looking north past the keep to the start of the descent from the ramparts to the River Colne below.

THE CASTLE GARDENS, 1904.
Much of this avenue survives in the outer bailey, although it's now bounded by 1920s' low walling, and the ornate benches have been replaced by more utilitarian ones. The trees have been thinned and the nicely restored bandstand is more visible.

CASTLE PARK, 1892.   31533

From the slopes below the Norman ditch and the avenue beyond, the park looks bleak and newly planted. Below can be seen Middle Mill, now demolished, and beyond the mill is the weir pool on the River Colne. The nearer pond is now the boating pool.

CASTLE PARK, 1907.   31532

The wall beyond the boating pool is part of the north defensive wall of the Roman town. Beyond were firstly Roman houses and then Anglo-Saxon: all cleared to make the outer bailey for the Norman castle. Behind are the tree-clad ramparts of the inner bailey along the ridge.

CASTLE PARK, CIVIL WAR SIEGE OBELISK, 1934.   86428

The obelisk was erected in 1892 on the site of the execution of two Royalist captains, Sir Charles Lucas and Sir George Lisle, on 28th August 1648. They were shot by order of Sir Thomas Fairfax, the Parliamentary general after the siege of the Civil War ended.

CASTLE GARDENS, 1934.

This sylvan path winds down from the castle inner bailey towards Park Lodge and then through the Roman wall to more open parkland with the boating pool and the River Colne. The path is much more open now and a little more municipalised.

THE PARK LODGE, *c.*1960.   C136027

The lodge was built before the Second World War in half-timbered style with a brick ground floor and effects the transition between the lower park, which was much more open, and the upper park which had many more mature trees and plantings.

THE BOATING POOL, 1904.   52352

Beyond the boating pool and outside the park was Middle Mill, demolished in the careless 1950s. The high chimney on the left belonged to a factory on the River Colne upstream from the watermill, and was also demolished.

THE BOATING POOL, *c.*1960.
The 1950s' boating-pool shelter still stands and the boats remain, still paddle boats. The thatched bowls pavilion in the distance was built in 1923 and gates into the park commemorate the park's opening by the Lord Mayor of London in October 1892.

THE TOWN FROM THE BOATING POOL, 1898.   41499
Looking across the boating pool, Jumbo the water tower can be seen, but work had only just started on the town hall so its great tower has not yet appeared. The foliage clump in the water is still here a hundred years later.

CHAPTER 4
PARISH CHURCHES & THE TOWN'S TWO ABBEYS

In the Domesday Book of 1086, Colchester is said to have seven priests. It can be assumed that this meant seven churches in the town. Of these only Holy Trinity retains Anglo-Saxon work in its tall mid-eleventh century tower and earlier nave west wall. St Botolph is a Saxon dedication and St Peter's is named. There was also St Runwald's in the high street, which survived until 1878.

In the later Middle Ages there were eight churches within the walls and more outside. Two of the greatest and most influential besides these were the monastic houses to the south of the walls. St John's Abbey was the richer of the two and a very prestigious Benedictine house, for its abbot sat in the House of Lords. It had been founded by Eudo Dapifer around 1096 and was dissolved in 1539, its last abbot being hanged. The abbey buildings or what remained of them were converted into a mansion which was destroyed in the 1648 siege. Only the gatehouse, a fine piece of fifteenth-century work, survives along with stretches of the precinct wall, notably along Mersea Road. The other monastery was St Botolph's Priory, of which the west part of the Norman nave survives. Again this suffered in the Civil War, the east part of the nave and doubtless other structures being cannoned out of existence.

Within the town walls many other parish churches suffered in the Civil-War siege, such as St Mary-at-the-Walls, whose tower had been used by Royalist snipers. This attracted Parliamentarian fire and all but the base of the tower was destroyed. Other churches suffered mishaps, such as St Peter's on North Hill, when an earthquake in 1692 severely damaged the tower. St Martin's also had the upper parts of its tower fall, while St Runwald in 1878 and St Nicholas in 1955 were demolished. By the eighteenth century the latter church had been a ruin, apart from its tower, but was restored and a dominating tower and spire added to the streetscape in 1876.

Several of the churches have Georgian work and some were extensively remodelled in Victorian times. In the case of St Mary-at-the-Walls, the Georgian work was demolished, apart from the tower, and rebuilt in harsh Victorian style.

The reduced population in the town centre led to various amalgamations of parish churches, a process that started in late-Victorian times. As a result several churches now have other uses: St Martin's became a cultural centre, All Saints a natural history museum, St Mary-at-the-Walls is the Colchester Arts Centre, St Giles is a Freemason's Lodge and Holy Trinity is a museum.

However the church buildings make a very important contribution to the character of the town and their towers, naves and chancels make a great impact. Often built in salvaged Roman brick and stone, or limestone and flint, they are set apart from the domestic scale of most of the other buildings. Not that the churches of Colchester are as grand as, say, many of those in Norwich or York, but they play a significant role in setting the style and character of Colchester as an historic town.

ALL SAINTS CHURCH, 1907.   57544

From the north the church, which is now a natural history museum, looks Victorian except for the fine early-sixteenth century west tower, but in fact the Norman nave south wall and fourteenth-century chancel are recognisable. Outside are the tram tracks and overhead wires for the system that only ran from 1904 until 1929.

ST PETER'S CHURCH, 1907.   57543

Its tower of 1758 in red brick with yellow brick quoins and battlements, the Georgianised aisles and the eighteenth-century galleries inside all disguise a medieval church. To add to the confusion, the Victorians added the clerestory and the curious lumpy clock with its medieval-style bracket and pediment.

St Martin's Church, 1921.

The late-seventeenth century tower with its liberal use of salvaged Roman brick fell in the seventeenth century. This fine church was closed in 1952, re-opened as a concert hall and theatre in 1958, but closed again. It still looks sad but repairs started in 1998 for a much-hoped-for re-opening.

60780

57

ST HELEN'S CHAPEL, 1892.
This thirteenth-century chapel has had a chequered career, having been a chantry chapel to 1530, a Quaker meeting house (1683-1800), a parish hall and now a museum store. The view of the castle was closed soon after this view by a pair of Edwardian cottages.

31536

59

HOLY TRINITY CHURCH, 1892.
The west tower, the church's most important feature, is Anglo-Saxon, mid-eleventh century and like many of the town's churches is built from salvage from the Roman town: bricks for arches, quoins and bands, and rubble and septaria (inferior stone nodules) for the rest. The nave west wall is also Anglo-Saxon.

31534

HOLY TRINITY CHURCH, WEST TOWER DOORWAY, 1892.   31535
The railings have now gone and the door is usable. It has a striking triangular arch, all in Roman brick, and characteristic of later Anglo-Saxon architecture. The wooden door itself is probably sixteenth century.

St Mary-at-the-Walls Church, 1904.

52356

Yet another parish church in secular use: this one is now the Colchester Arts Centre. Most of the church was rebuilt in 1872, while the tower is part fifteenth century, part 1729, replacing what had been destroyed in the 1648 Siege. The current battlements were added in 1911.

ST MARY-AT-THE-WALLS CHURCH, 1904.   57546
Sir Arthur Blomfields's hard brick 1872 church replaced a brick one of 1713-14, which itself had replaced the
medieval building destroyed in the 1648 siege. Apparently the church had been used by snipers, one of them
one-eyed(!), and thus attracted Parliamentary bombardment.

ST JOHN'S ABBEY GATEHOUSE, 1921.   70364
Of Eudo Dapifer's great abbey foundation in 1096, only the fifteenth-century gatehouse and some of the precinct
walls survive, the rest having been bombarded during the 1648 Siege. The gatehouse itself, with its superb
flushwork decoration, gives an idea of the medieval abbey's power and wealth.

ST BOTOLPH'S PRIORY AND CHURCH, 1907.   57539

Like St John's Abbey, St Botolph's Priory lay outside the town walls. It was founded before 1100, but never grew
very large. Looking beyond the west front of the nave, the present St Botolph's church of 1837 is in neo-Norman
style and built in white brick.

St Botolph's Priory Nave, 1892

31528

Dissolved as a priory under Henry VIII in 1535, the church had been used as the town corporation church, but the 1648 Siege converted it into the romantic, ivy-clad ruin seen in this view. In 1912 repairs and consolidation started, and the church attained its present appearance.

St Botolph's Priory Nave, 1892.   31529
Within the nave, centuries of burials had raised the ground level by about 4ft and this view shows the tombs, surrounded by railings, which were removed in 1912, when the ground level was lowered to Norman pavement level and the tombs reinstated.

ST BOTOLPH'S PRIORY, THE WEST DOORWAY, 1892.   31527
This view through the great west door with limestone in the arches shows the building materials well: Roman
bricks, septaria and flint. Originally of course, like Norman St Alban's Abbey, the walls were plastered or rendered
and limewashed, then painted to mimic fine stonework blocks.

ST LEONARD'S CHURCH, LEXDEN, 1895.
Originally a separate village, Lexden is now absorbed in Colchester's south-western expansion, but its identity is still clear with the church at its heart. The nave is of 1820 and cement-rendered, and the flint chancel dates from 1894. The robust memorial drinking fountain dates from 1893.

35508

Chapter 5

The River Colne from Colchester to Wivenhoe

The River Colne has always played a crucial role in the history of Colchester. Well before the Roman conquest it had defended the north and east flanks of the capital of Cymbeline's kingdom, while the west flank was protected by a series of dykes and ramparts, some of which run south from the river. Long stretches of these Iron-Age defensive works survive on either side of Lexden and were clearly intended to protect the west and south-west flanks of the town.

To the Romans the river also had a defensive function but it was a vital trade artery too, as it had been in pre-Roman years. Fingringhoe was the port for the Roman supply ships and later their traders, although the ships soon moved upstream to Old Heath. "Heath" is a later corruption of Hythe, Anglo-Saxon for a haven or harbour.

In medieval times the cloth trade developed from Colchester and the port moved to Hythe, then known as New Hythe. Here the port of Colchester had developed by the twelfth century with its own parish church, St Leonards-at-the-Hythe. The quayside buildings have been rebuilt numerous times and virtually none survive from before the nineteenth century.

The trade at Hythe flourished until eclipsed by the railways, but has revived more recently. There has been much rebuilding and the quays are lined with sheet-metal piling. It is a thriving, busy port and industrial and warehousing site.

In Colchester the watermills that drew their power from the river have either been demolished like Middle Mill, or have found new uses, like Marriage's Mill by East Street which is now the Colchester Mill Hotel. Industrial development grew up alongside the river bank, particularly on the south bank between North Bridge and Middle Mill, but all these concerns have been rebuilt in the last 20 years.

The River Colne is now a beautiful river flowing around the town with riverside paths. Going through parks, its recreational function is predominant. Two miles downstream from Hythe is Wivenhoe, a small town whose historic core is alongside the river, but whose hinterland of modern development spreads a mile inland. By the river there are typical late-eighteenth and early-nineteenth century riverside houses and terraces, many with bow and bay windows to take advantage of their setting. Immediately in front of them is the quay and boats. There are also small nineteenth-century warehouses and ship-building sheds. This maritime business carries on to this day and there are still boat builders and repairers and boatyards.

A small distance from the quay is Anchor Hill and the parish church. Beyond is High Street and the railway. Wivenhoe retains the charm of a small port and riverside town or, rather, large village and is a popular spot. It looks particularly attractive from across or on the river, with the varied Georgian river-front houses and warehouses, and the church tower of about 1500 with its charming cupola peeping over the river-front houses.

RIVER COLNE, UPSTREAM FROM NORTH BRIDGE, 1904.   52354
North Bridge crosses the River Colne on the line of North Hill/Head Street, which still follows one of the main
roads of the Roman town. This view looks upstream from the latest bridge past what was the Castle Inn and is now
the Riverside Hotel and Restaurant.

RIVER COLNE, DOWNSTREAM FROM NORTH BRIDGE, 1895.   35506
The south bank of the Colne has been industrialised for centuries, but all the buildings in this view have gone, to be
replaced by less-attractive modern industrial and commercial buildings. The riverside walk now follows both banks
of the river.

MIDDLE MILL WEIR, *c.*1960.
Until the 1950s Middle Mill Weir occupied the centre of this view, but the bridge over the weir remains as an important pedestrian link to the sportsfields and parks on the north bank of the River. They preserve some feeling of the countryside reaching the town.

CASTLE GARDENS, RIVER COLNE, 1904.
Looking towards Middle Mill, the more-rural feel of the river banks is captured well. The river now flows between manicured banks and sadly the John Constable-esque tree has gone.

HYTHE QUAY, *c.*1960.   C136062

The quay may have been the port of Roman Colchester and certainly from the Middle Ages it handled the town's trade. The medieval village was slightly inland from the quay, now lined by sheet piles and surprisingly bustling, although the splendid sailing barges which survived into the 1960s have long gone.

WIVENHOE QUAY, *c.*1960.   W160054

This small and delightful riverside town has a bustling quayside with a mix of pleasure boats and commerce in the shape of boat builders and repairers. Warehouses and cottages line the quay, many of them Georgian and early-nineteenth century with many picturesque bow windows to take advantage of the river views.

WIVENHOE QUAY AND RIVER COLNE, *c.*1960.
Little has changed in the last 40 years with similar boats still berthed, although the woods across the river are thinner and the view of the ballast works is now more intrusive beyond the crane.

VIEW FROM WIVENHOE QUAY, *c.*1960.   W160056
These charming houses are at the east end of the quay and the left-hand one, Ferry House, is a reminder of the Colne ferry that crossed the river here. To the right are the cranes of a boatyard.

ANCHOR HILL, *c.*1955.   W160017
Just inland is Anchor Hill, a small square surrounded by cottages and shops with the church behind the delicatessen. Further along a lane to the right, East Street, is Garrison House whose upper floor is a virtuoso display of mid-seventeenth century "pargetting" or decorative plasterwork.

HIGH STREET, c.1955.

Beyond Anchor Hill the high street passes the churchyard with its gatepiers and gates presented by Eliza Howard in 1901. The church was damaged in the 1884 earthquake that also damaged parts of Colchester. The gap in the middle distance is the bridge over the railway line in its cutting.

W16011

Pictorial Memories Collection

A great new range of publications featuring the work of innovative Victorian photographer Francis Frith.

⊗ 1998 Titles ⊗

County Series   £9.99

1-84125-045-7	Berkshire	
053-8	Buckinghamshire	
024-4	Derbyshire	
077-5	Greater London	
028-7	Kent	
029-5	Lake District	
051-1	Lancashire	
031-7	Leicestershire	
026-0	London	
027-9	Norfolk	
030-9	Sussex	
063-5	West Yorkshire	
025-2	Yorkshire	

Town & City Series   £9.99

010-4	Brighton & Hove	
015-5	Canterbury	
079-1	Edinburgh	
012-0	Glasgow & Clydeside	
081-3	Norwich	
040-6	York	

Country Series   £9.99

1-84125-075-9	Ireland	
071-6	North Wales	
073-2	Scotland	
069-4	South Wales	

Poster Books   £4.99

000-7	Canals and Waterways	
032-5	Derbyshire	
001-5	High Days and Holidays	
036-8	Kent	
037-6	Lake District	
034-1	London	
005-8	Railways	

£5.99

023-6	Canterbury	
043-0	Derby	

⊗ Titles from January to July 1999 ⊗

County Series   £9.99

1-84125-049-x	Warwickshire	March
047-3	Staffordshire	
057-0	Devon	
067-8	Cheshire	
065-1	Nottinghamshire	
059-7	Cornwall	

1-84125-101-1	Surrey	
095-3	Hampshire	
128-3	Highlands	April
149-6	Hertfordshire	
130-5	North Yorkshire	May
150-x	Wiltshire	

Town & City Series   £7.99

089-9	Maidstone	March
087-2	Bradford	
083-x	Colchester	
093-7	Dublin	
091-0	Leeds	
105-4	Buxton	
111-9	Bristol	
113-7	Nottingham	
011-2	Manchester	
107-0	Matlock	
009-0	Macclesfield	April
132-1	St Ives	
008-2	Derby	
133-x	Sevenoaks	
014-7	Newbury	
134-8	Bognor Regis	
144-5	Leicester	
145-3	East Grinstead	
146-1	Newark	

137-2	Sheffield	May
138-0	Cambridge	
139-9	Penzance	
140-2	Eastbourne	
147-x	Llandudno	
142-9	Torquay	
148-8	Whitby	
159-3	Scarborough	June
160-7	Faversham to Herne Bay	
164-x	Scilly Isles	
162-3	Dorset Coast	
168-2	Falmouth	
165-8	Newquay	
154-2	Bakewell	July
163-1	Lincoln	
167-4	Barnstaple	
174-7	Great Yarmouth	
141-0	Blackpool	
207-7	Dartmoor	

WATERTON PRESS, WATERTON ESTATE, BRIDGEND, GLAMORGAN, CF31 3XP.
TEL: 01656 668836   FAX: 01656 668710

BLACKPOOL, 1906